Read-About® Geography

West Virginia

By Susan Labella

Subject Consultant
Joseph J. Kerski, Geographer
U.S. Geological Survey
Denver, Colorado

Reading Consultant
Cecilia Minden–Cupp, PhD
Former Director of the Language and Literacy Program
Harvard Graduate School of Education
Cambridge, Massachusetts

Children's Press®
A Division of Scholastic Inc.
New York   Toronto   London   Auckland   Sydney
Mexico City   New Delhi   Hong Kong
Danbury, Connecticut

Designer: Herman Adler Design
Photo Researcher: Caroline Anderson
The photo on the cover shows the New River Gorge in West Virginia.

Library of Congress Cataloging-in-Publication Data

Labella, Susan, 1948–
  West Virginia / by Susan Labella.
     p. cm. — (Rookie Read-About Geography)
  Includes index.
  ISBN 0-516-24994-0 (lib. bdg.)   0-516-26456-7 (pbk.)
  1. West Virginia—Juvenile literature. 2. West Virginia—Geography—
Juvenile literature. I. Title. II. Series.
  F241.3.L33 2006
  917.54'02—dc22   2005021640

CHILDREN'S PRESS, and ROOKIE READ-ABOUT®,
and associated logos are trademarks and/or registered trademarks
of Scholastic Library Publishing. SCHOLASTIC and associated logos
are trademarks and/or registered trademarks of Scholastic Inc.

1 2 3 4 5 6 7 8 9 10 R 15 14 13 12 11 10 09 08 07 06

Which state is the
Mountain State?

It's West Virginia!

West Virginia is on
the eastern side of the
United States.

Can you find West
Virginia on this map?

CANADA

WASHINGTON

OREGON

IDAHO

MONTANA

WYOMING

NORTH DAKOTA

SOUTH DAKOTA

MINNESOTA

WISCONSIN

MICHIGAN

NEW HAMPSHIRE

VERMONT

MAINE

NEVADA

UTAH

COLORADO

NEBRASKA

IOWA

ILLINOIS

INDIANA

OHIO

NEW YORK

PENNSYLVANIA

MASSACHUSETTS

RHODE ISLAND

CONNECTICUT

NEW JERSEY

DELAWARE

MARYLAND

Washington, D.C.

CALIFORNIA

ARIZONA

NEW MEXICO

KANSAS

MISSOURI

WEST VIRGINIA

VIRGINIA

KENTUCKY

NORTH CAROLINA

OKLAHOMA

ARKANSAS

TENNESSEE

SOUTH CAROLINA

TEXAS

MISSISSIPPI

ALABAMA

GEORGIA

LOUISIANA

FLORIDA

ALASKA

CANADA

MEXICO

HAWAII

North

West

East

South

5

The Allegheny Mountains

The Allegheny and
Blue Ridge mountains
run through part of
West Virginia.

The Blue Ridge Mountains

People like to hike or ride
bikes on the mountain trails.

In the winter, West Virginia's mountains are great for skiing.

10

Spruce Knob Mountain is the highest point in West Virginia. From the top, you can usually see all the way to Virginia. That is the next state to the east.

A lot of caves lie underneath
West Virginia's mountains.
People like to explore
these caves.

13

West Virginia has underground coal mines, too. Many people in West Virginia work for coal companies.

Coal is burned to give off heat. Coal is also burned to help make electricity. Most of West Virginia's electricity comes from burning coal.

During the summer heat, people in West Virginia head for the water. They love to go white-water rafting on West Virginia's rivers.

Many types of birds, flowers, and trees live along West Virginia's rivers.

The cardinal is West Virginia's state bird.

The rhododendron is West
Virginia's state flower.

The sugar maple is West Virginia's state tree.

The capital of West
Virginia is Charleston.
It is also the largest city
in the state.

West Virginia is the
41st-largest state in the
United States.

PENNSYLVANIA

OHIO

Ohio River

MARYLAND

**WEST
VIRGINIA**

Kanawha River

⭐ Charleston

Allegheny Mountains

△ *Spruce Knob Mountain*

VIRGINIA

KENTUCKY

North
West ✦ East
South

SCALE 1 inch = 50 miles

0	Miles	50

0	Kilometers	80

Boats at Charleston's river festival

Every year, Charleston holds a large river festival. People come to the Kanawha River to watch boat races.

There's a lot to do in West Virginia.

Go and see for yourself!

Words You Know

Allegheny Mountains

Blue Ridge Mountains

30

cardinal

coal mines

rhododendron

white-water rafting

Index

About the Author

Susan Labella is a freelance writer. She is the author of other books in the Rookie Read-About® Geography series.

Photo Credits

Photographs © 2006: Alamy Images/Jim West: 7, 30 bottom; Corbis Images: 23 (William A. Bake), 14, 31 top right (Ed Eckstein), 10 (David Muench); Danita Delimont Stock Photography: 18, 31 bottom right (Lynn Seldon), cover, 6, 30 top (Stephen J. Shaluta, Jr.); Folio, Inc.: 13 (Skip Brown), 22, 31 bottom left (John Moss); Getty Images/Jeremy Woodhouse/Photodisc Green: 21, 31 top left; Index Stock Imagery/Pat Canova: 9; Photri Inc./Steve J. Shaluta: 29; Superstock, Inc./Robert Llewellyn: 17; The Image Works/Jeff Greenberg: 8; WV Tourism/Steve J. Shaluta: 3, 26.

Maps by Bob Italiano